450
Low-Cost
No-Cost
Strategies
for recognizing,
rewarding & retaining
good people

By: Carol A. Hacker

Carol A. Hacker & Associates
209 Cutty Sark Way
Alpharetta, Georgia 30005
PHONE - 770-410-0517
FAX - 770-667-9801

Gaonmind@aol.com
CarolAHacker@hotmail.com

ISBN 0-9662011-1-6

This publication is designed to provide accurate and authoritative information in regarded to the subject matter covered. It is sold with the understanding that neither the author nor the publisher is engaged in rendering legal, accounting, or other professional service. If legal advice or other expert assistance is required, the services of a competent professional should be sought.

From a Declaration of Principles jointly adopted by a Committee of the American Bar Association and a Committee of Publishers.

Printed in the United States of America.

Contents

Acknowledgments

Many people have contributed to the success of this book. Thank you Gerry and Kaye Durnell for giving me the opportunity to speak at Pizza Expo. This all started with you and the hundreds of pizza restaurant owners and managers who attended my workshop on this subject in Las Vegas in 1997. They graciously submitted their best ideas for keeping good people. Many were simple, low-cost/no-cost suggestions that work for them.

Special thanks to Bill Coffman, a great manager and friend. People love working for you because you truly care. Thank you Bill and Cher Holton. You are the most talented couple I know, and not just on the dance floor! Thank you Virginia, my mother, for encouraging me and contributing suggestions for this book.

Judy Rogers, you're the best editor and friend in the world. I marvel at your gift for writing. You're the angel who looks out for me as I find my way in the literary world. "Thank you" never seems like enough.

Business owners, managers and supervisors generously shared ideas. Employees who benefited from their company's interest and creativity in recognizing them for good performance have also contributed to this endeavor. To the many other people who offered suggestions for this book, thank you. May you always continue to find ways to keep your employees happy and proud to be on your team!

About the Author

Carol A. Hacker is an educator, speaker and the founder of Carol A. Hacker & Associates, one of the country's foremost skill-building enterprises for human resource management. For more than two decades she's been a significant voice in front-line and corporate human resource management to Fortune 500 companies as well as small businesses. She ranks among the experts in the field of recruiting and retention issues. With hands-on experience in managing a wide variety of public, private and non-profit consulting and training projects, her client list spans North America and Europe.

A graduate of the University of Wisconsin, Carol earned her B.S. and M.S. with honors. Prior to starting her own firm in January 1989, she held a number of management positions including that of Director of Human Resources for the North American Division of Bahlsen Inc., a multi-million dollar European manufacturer.

She's the author of *The Costs of Bad Hiring Decisions & How to Avoid Them (St. Lucie Press, 1996), The High Cost of Low Morale ...and what to do about it (St. Lucie Press, 1997), The Costs of Bad Hiring Decisions & How to Avoid Them, 2nd Edition (St. Lucie Press, 1998), Hiring Top Performers-350 Great Interview Questions For People Who Need People (1998 revised), Job Hunting in the 21st Century-Exploding the Myths, Exploring the Realities (St. Lucie Press, 1999), 366 Surefire Ways to Let Your Employees Know They Count (InSync Communications, 2000),* and dozens of published articles.

Carol's also a member of the National Speakers Association, and speaks to professional and trade associations, as well as to private corporations and government agencies. She draws on her strong business background to tailor management training programs for organizations of all sizes. Her motivational presentations are practical, positive and entertaining. Her interactive workshops have helped thousands of managers become better leaders.

Some of her most popular workshops include:

- How to Compete in the War for Talent
- How to Take the Guesswork Out of Interviewing
- How to Hire Top Performers
- Keeping Winners
- 21st Century Strategies for Gaining Employee Loyalty and Reducing Turnover
- How to Conduct "Win-Win" Performance Appraisals

Introduction

Many business owners and managers overlook the use of low-cost or no-cost incentives as a way to encourage and retain their employees. Why? Some think that recognizing or honoring people means spending a lot of money. Not true! Others believe they're paying employees to do a job and therefore should not have to acknowledge their achievements.

Low unemployment, combined with increasingly aggressive recruiting has made keeping good people more and more difficult. The issue isn't simply losing a key member of your team—there's also the hassle and cost of finding a replacement. Businesses that are able to keep motivated employees, who in turn produce satisfied and loyal customers, have a strategic, competitive advantage and are usually successful.

If you want to keep winning employees, there are two points to consider that may cost you some money, but have the potential to pay dividends for years to come. There's no getting around it; compensation and benefits are important to most people and shouldn't be overlooked.

1. Is the compensation competitive? Money is a powerful tool that includes sign-on bonuses, retention rewards, annual lump-sum payments for employees nearing the end of their salary grade, and market-based adjustments to the salary structure.

2. Have you considered making benefits flexible? Have you considered stock purchase plans, stock options, long-term care insurance, legal insurance and financial planning benefits? How about reimbursement for an Executive MBA program?

This book contains dozens of low-cost/no-cost ideas for rewarding good performance, and building fun into your organization. Many of the ideas have been used before; others are new but are currently being successfully implemented in organizations of all types throughout North America.

Principles

Behind the success of any thriving business are a number of principles related to keeping good people. Mary Kay Ash, founder of Mary Kay Cosmetics, said it well: "There are two things people want more than sex and money—recognition and praise." With that light-hearted but powerful thought, I'd like to share some basic principles for recognizing and rewarding your employees while making it fun to work for you.

♦ For any reward system to have an impact on performance, it must be part of a work environment that's rewarding as a whole.

♦ Keep in mind the generation gap—what employees appreciated twenty years ago, may seem ridiculous today. Reward employees accordingly.

♦ Reward people by allowing them to get involved. Encouraging them to make decisions increases the likelihood of compliance with your requests.

♦ *Isolated* reinforcement of specific behavior has little motivational impact. It must be on-going in order to be effective.

♦ Use of fear, intimidation, threats and power of authority may be a way to get attention, but these often meet with resistance, reluctance and animosity.

♦ Find ways to make people feel important and appreciated. Teach your managers how to nurture employee loyalty. Be a good listener. Be tolerant and show understanding. Handle resistance with patience, harmony and honesty. Let others be themselves.

♦ When people are free to laugh, they begin to relax. They begin to care. Laughter fuels creativity so people can perform at their best.

♦ "If you want 1 year of prosperity, grow grain. If you want 10 years of prosperity, grow trees. If you want 100 years of prosperity, grow people." —Chinese Proverb

Chapter 1 - Recognition

You don't have to wait for employees to win an award or do something that merits special attention before recognizing them in a significant way. Everyone likes to feel noticed at times and such things as remembering an employee's birthday or taking a moment to say "thanks" can mean more to someone than many managers realize. Let people know that you value them both as employees and as individuals. Here are some ideas to help you recognize accomplishments:

1. Name a special award after an employee such as a safety award, production award, years of service award, community service award or even a scholarship.

2. Design a poster honoring an outstanding employee.

3. Arrange for the company president to meet with each new employee, regardless of position, for one hour within the first month on the job.

4. Recognize new employees by painting their names on coffee mugs. Have the mugs waiting for them on their desks on the day they start work.

5. Acknowledge birthdays with a note of congratulations, cake, or balloon bouquet.

6. Present an employee with a birthday card on his or her birthday that's signed by everyone in the department.

7. Hold an "Employee Recognition" day or week. If for a week, have a small surprise each day.

8. Create an "Oscar® Award" with several categories. Hold an awards night with employees as the emcees. Employees might also provide entertainment between awards.

9. Let the employee know that you're putting a note in his or her personnel file to document exceptional performance.

10. Arrange to have a star in the galaxy named after an employee.

11. Honor employees' special achievements using an electronic bulletin board.

12. Promote your superstars ahead of schedule.

13. Create a "walk of fame" hallway. Print the names of your employees to be recognized on adhesive footprints and adhere them to the floor in a highly visible area of the company.

14. Write a personal note to employees on the back of their paycheck envelope every time they're paid. Seal with a yellow smiley face sticker.

15. Recognize employees for their hard work with a classified ad in the local newspaper. Consider mentioning the names of each employee in the ad. Go one step further and include a photo of the entire team along with a few words of "thanks" or congratulations.

16. Send a thank you letter to the employees' children. The text might say something like: "Please accept my sincere appreciation for the support you have given to your mother (dad) in her (his) pursuit of a career with our company. I'm fortunate to have her (him) on the team and want you to know how lucky you are to have her (him) as your parent." This letter could also be adapted for a spouse, or the spouse and children of an employee.

17. Dedicate special parking places for peak performers based on measurable accomplishments. Rotate monthly or quarterly.

18. Keep employees involved with the business at hand. Use adhesive foil stars at staff meetings as recognition. When someone offers a helpful suggestion, gets everyone laughing, or has a great idea, anyone at the meeting may award that person with a star. An individual may also award him or herself with a star.

19. Hold periodic standing ovations to recognize special achievements or when a team meets its goals.

20. Save old calendar pages from desk top calendars such as Gary Larson's "Far Side" or John Gray's "Men are from Mars, Women are from Venus." When writing a note of appreciation to an employee, write it on one of the calendar pages that comes closest to fitting the occasion.

21. Greet all employees with a smile and call them by name.

22. Thank employees for their efforts in front of their peers.

23. Send flowers or a gift certificate to the employee's spouse.

24. Pass out "Kudo®" candy bars for a job well done.

25. Name a product you manufacture after an employee who has had a significant achievement.

26. Recognize an employee for a "life saving" idea with a necklace made from Lifesavers®.

27. Throw a party to celebrate when an employee becomes a U.S. citizen.

28. When an employee earns a patent, put the first page of the patent on a plaque and present it to the employee in a ceremony in front of his or her peers.

29. Invite honored employees to have lunch with the president or owner of the company.

30. Recognize those who volunteer in their community with a Community Service Award. (See Chapter 7 for specific ideas).

31. Recognize diversity. Glue a large map of the world on bulletin board material and hang it on the wall. Employees who have lived in a country other than the United States get to put a long pin on the city in the country where they lived. This is a great way to recognize the diversity that your employees bring to the workplace.

32. Pin or tape paper streamers to the ceiling of the office or plant to recognize and celebrate each goal the team hits.

33. Have the CEO send a personalized note to a new employee at the end of his or her first week on the job.

34. Name a menu item in the company cafeteria in honor of an employee.

35. Recognize an employee by having the company cafeteria prepare a favorite recipe provided by the employee.

36. Send a memo to the employee's supervisor's supervisor about the great job the employee is doing.

37. Vote for "Employee of the Month." Let each employee have two votes so they can vote once for themselves if they choose to do so.

38. Make a donation to the humane society in the name of the employee's pet(s). Preferably the pet is not deceased!

39. Throw a surprise "this is your life" party for the employee(s) in recognition of special achievements, retirement or just for fun.

40. Decorate his or her work area on the employee's birthday. The entire team may want to get involved in creating this birthday fun day.

41. Australian Body Works of Atlanta, a health club, offers a "Spot an Eagle in Flight" award. "Eagle of the Moment" is a program that allows their members to recognize employees. Cards are available to fill out and turn into the Member Services desk when a member spots "an eagle in flight."

42. Consider the "I'll Find A Way" recognition program. Employees share stories in staff meetings about co-workers who have gone out of their way for customers.

43. Recognize the most energetic employee of the month in front of his or her peers with an Energizer® battery.

44. Have the president or a high-ranking member of the company telephone an employee in your department and thank him or her for a particularly outstanding accomplishment.

45. Recognize employees when they receive their GED, high school diploma, college degree, or a special certification or license such as CPA.

46. Support a "Roving Recognition Band" as does Tricon Global Restaurants, Inc., in Louisville, Kentucky. Kazoos buzz, plastic noisemakers shriek and cowbells clang to shatter an early morning calm at corporate headquarters. Band employees, in casual dress, drop in on other employees they've been told deserve an extra pat on the back for a great job. The band is one method they use to "rev up" their 750,000 employees.

47. Kentucky Fried Chicken regularly hands out rubber chickens to top performers. At Pizza Hut, Inc. they hand out big chunks of fake cheese. At Taco Bell Corp., it's a giant papier-mâché chili pepper.

48. Write a year-end letter to your employees, sharing the department's successes for the year. Include something about everyone on the team. Part of the text might say: "Let me express my sincere thanks to the entire team for the dedicated and skilled work that was performed throughout the year. We couldn't have reached our goal without everyone's help. Here are some examples of your major accomplishments…"

49. ProTech Publishing and Communications, Inc. in New Albany, Indiana, holds a "Are You a Pizza Giraffe?" recognition award for people who help those in need in the community. Example: Employee earns money for a local charity by sponsoring a Special Olympics team, or raises awareness for a particular cause. Pizza Giraffes—those who go the extra mile—are regularly featured in their industry magazine, *Pizza Today*. Magazine subscribers, most of whom are pizza operators, make the nominations.

50. When a Boy Scout earns his Eagle Scout award or a military reservist is promoted, have the entire staff turn out to celebrate the employee's accomplishment.

51. Hold monthly anniversary lunches where everyone hired during that month is recognized for his or her contributions to the organization.

52. Welcome new hires by being prepared for their first day on the job. Make sure the workspace has office supplies, software loaded on their computers, and a name plate placed on their desk. Show them restrooms, break rooms, the cafeteria and how to use the telephone. Don't assume someone else has taken care of these things. Helping new employees get off on the right foot is critical to keeping them for the long haul.

53. Kitchen staff needs recognition too. One hotel gives out "Golden Knife" awards for exemplary performance over a specified period of time. The knife is made of fancy steel and brass and engraved with the employee's name and time period of award (in this case, monthly). The knives are displayed in a trophy case adjacent to the hotel bar.

54. Designate a wall as the "Employee Wall of Fame." Post customer appreciation letters that recognize your employees for a great job or for going out of their way to serve a customer.

55. Refer to all employees as "associates" instead of "employees."

56. Celebrate moments of success using confetti and horns. Employees "hoot and holler" for 60 seconds in recognition of their team's accomplishments.

57. After an especially busy week, put Hershey Kisses® on everyone's desk before they arrive at work on Friday morning to recognize extra effort.

58. Schedule a 5-minute break during which everyone says something nice to a co-worker.

59. Make Monday mornings special by doing something to recognize your employees at the start of the week.

60. Name conference rooms after long-term employees. The name plate remains above the door of the room until the employee retires.

Chapter 2 - Awards/Rewards

An <u>award</u> is defined as something that is conferred or bestowed. Awards are usually given when an employee reaches a goal, wins a contest, or is part of a team that reaches a significant milestone.

In addition to big awards, consider giving smaller awards throughout the year. Set specific criteria that employees must meet to earn these awards. Make the awards available on an on-going basis so employees celebrate moments of achievement throughout the year, not just at the year-end awards ceremony.

A <u>reward</u> is something that is given as recognition. In addition to using rewards as an incentive for employees to meet specific goals, consider rewarding employees for day-to-day excellence. Reward them for rising to the occasion when a crisis occurs or they're asked to work unexpected overtime. Maybe an employee voluntarily came in on the weekend because he or she took the initiative and recognized the importance of a particular project. Tie rewards to effort rather than success or failure.

Some of the award and reward ideas are things the employee would be aware of in advance, such as paying a referral bonus to an individual who recommends someone and the new hire remains for at least 90 or 180 days. Still others should be spontaneous—something the employee isn't expecting, which will be all the more pleasantly surprising and appreciated. For example, surprise employees who have completed a long, hard and demanding project with an extra day of vacation or dinner at a nice restaurant. Let your employees know you appreciate their day-to-day work as well as the "big deals."

1. Award a gift certificate to a health spa or for a facial, manicure or color analysis.

2. Award a free round of golf with the company president at his or her country club.

3. The "white lab coat" award: A white (or any color you choose) lab coat is awarded to the employee with the most helpful cost-saving idea of the month. The lab coat rotates every month (with laundry service provided).

4. Award an on-line gift certificate. For example, the on-line book retailer www.amazon.com issues gift certificates through its Web site. Another Web site is www.webcertificate.com. Select the denomination, choose a design and include a personal message. Then send the certificate instantly over the Internet. The recipient can spend it at one or several on-line stores until the credit limit is depleted. Be aware of expiration dates on all gift certificates.

5. Award gift certificates to the CD exchange store.

6. Award a gift certificate to a video rental store such as Blockbuster.

7. Let an employee use your vehicle or boat for a day.

8. Award movie passes for the "best showing" in your business. Let employees define what the "best showing" means.

9. Do away with performance appraisals, but give regular, verbal performance feedback.

10. Have employees write their own job descriptions and find out what your employees are really doing.

11. Encourage employees to write their own job titles. One creative employee calls himself a "software gardener."

12. Reward with a gift certificate for a free car wash and wax.

13. Reward with special bonuses. It doesn't have to be a large sum of money. If it's unexpected, it's even better.

14. Award a gift certificate for a one-time house cleaning by a professional service.

15. Award gift certificates to fast food restaurants. Some restaurants will give gift certificates free of charge to employers if you ask.

16. Award compensatory time off.

17. Award with a prepaid telephone card.

18. When they reach a goal, surprise your employees with an extra 15-minute break.

19. Award with a "Scratch and Win" card of company design. Employees scratch off company logo and win one of many small gift items such as a soft drink, a bag of chips, roll of Lifesavers®, a candy bar, pack of gum, or any typical vending machine item. The dollar value of the item isn't important; it's the fun of scratching and winning that employees like.

20. Award the executive privilege of an extra 15 minutes for lunch.

21. Award a gift certificate for dry cleaning.

22. Award employees with portable hand tools such as an electric drill, power screwdriver, Skill® saw, wrench or socket set.

23. Award U.S. Savings Bonds. There's no commission or fee and you can buy one for as little as $25.00. For questions contact the Savings Bond Operations Office at 304-480-6112.

24. Add money to an employee's retirement account.

25. Provide a "pull board." For every 150 contracts keyed, or telephone calls answered, employees get to pull one ticket off the board. They can exchange tickets for prizes or cash awards.

26. Implement a "Star of the Month" award where employees vote for the individual who went the extra mile for a co-worker or customer.

27. Award gift certificates for $5 through $25 in a drawing for employees who have perfect attendance for the month.

28. Contribute toward the cost of tutoring services for employees who have children with special needs.

29. Make it worthwhile for employees to save their sick days. Allow them to bank sick days and use them to reduce the cost of health insurance benefits to the employee in retirement, or reduce premiums on current insurance.

30. Award an automobile CD player.

31. Consider an American Express Gift Cheque. It's a gift certificate that can be used virtually anywhere. The checks are available in $25, $50 and $100 denominations, and come in a gold envelope with a gift card. There's a $2.50 charge for each check, regardless of denomination. They're replaceable if lost or stolen. You can buy American Express Gift Cheques at many banks, or by calling 1-800-828-4438.

32. Let an employee set his or her own schedule for the week.

33. Reward an employee with an opportunity to be in a company radio or television commercial, or at least, to observe the recording or filming of the commercial.

34. Reward a group of employees (and/or their children) with the opportunity to ride on a company float in a community parade.

35. Reward employees with cards and small gift items from a store that offers motivational products such as Successories®.

36. Have fruit, chocolate, nuts, jellies or jams delivered monthly to an employee's home for a specified period of time.

37. Give a bookstore gift certificate.

38. Reward employees with a personalized pair of Levi® jeans. For $55, consumers can design jeans with the precise Levi's models, leg openings, colors, sizes, zippers or buttons they want. Orders are usually filled within two weeks.

39. Pay for dues in a professional association.

40. Pay for a professional association magazine subscription.

41. Throw a party for everyone who retires. Also, consider sponsoring a retirees club that meets monthly.

42. Award all employees a specific amount of "well" days in lieu of "sick" days.

43. Give the "Diaper Award" (a diaper with the company logo on it) to new parents.

44. Allow an employee the privilege of flexing his or her work schedule for a specified amount of time.

45. Reward with a three-day weekend with the third day paid.

46. Reward with a magazine subscription of the employee's choice.

47. Reward with karate, skating, skiing, golfing or dance lessons for employees or their children.

48. Give the gift of time with a watch; consider a sports watch with the company logo or a message on the face of the watch.

49. Pay for one week of childcare.

50. Arrange for an executive level employee to spend one-half day with an employee doing the employee's job.

51. Provide an all expense paid trip for an employee to the annual shareholders' meeting.

52. Pay for one month of elder care services for an employee's family member.

53. Reward with two tickets to a sporting or theatre event.

54. Offer the executive privilege of arriving at work five minutes late and leaving five minutes early.

55. Anonymously, have a pizza, cake, balloons or flowers delivered to an employee or team of employees for reaching a significant goal.

56. Offer a modified sabbatical where a modest amount of money is paid to the employee and/or insurance premium is paid in full while he or she is on a leave of absence.

57. Reward with lottery tickets.

58. For the business traveler, reward with an upgrade from a hotel room to a suite.

59. Each month, provide bagels, donuts and coffee or tea for all employees on the teams that reach their goals.

60. Award "gift selector catalogs." Catalogs can be given for increased production, sales contests, perfect attendance, service awards, retirement gifts, safety awards, or employee of the month. Employees can select from many gift items featured in the catalogs.

61. In an elementary school, the PTO/PTA recognizes teachers twice each year with a salad luncheon on their in-service days.

62. Reward performers employees with the complimentary use of an income tax preparation service.

63. Take a break every 6 months and take your team for an off-site meeting.

64. Award a month's supply of food for the employee's pet.

65. Pay for a one time grooming of the employee's pet.

66. As an on-the-spot reward, tell the employee to take a break for one hour while you take over his or her job.

67. You may not have the authority to give one of your employees a day off with pay. However, surprise the employee on your day off by showing up and telling him or her to go home, that you are working in his or her place, *and*, that the offer expires in five minutes if they don't leave immediately.

68. Silver commemorative coins are unusual gifts, beautiful keepsakes and works of art. Many commemoratives have themes that make them special. For example, the Black Revolutionary Patriots coin set salutes Crispus Attucks, who was killed in the Boston Massacre of 1770. A portion of the proceeds may go to the construction of the Black Patriots Memorial on the National Mall in Washington, D.C. The proof commemorative silver dollar costs $37.00. The U.S. Mint also offers commemorative coins honoring Dolly Madison, Robert F. Kennedy and the National Law Enforcement Officers Memorial. For a U.S. Mint catalogue call 1-800-872-6468 or try them on the Internet at www.usmint.gov.

69. Reward with a gift card, such as that offered by First USA. The plastic, prepaid cards are available in any amount, starting at $50.00. Each time the recipient uses the card, the purchase amount is deducted from it. The cards come in 11 designs and bear the recipient's name and a personal greeting of up to 19 characters. They can be used anywhere a Visa credit card is accepted. To order call: 1-888-378-4438.

70. The Embassy Suites Phoenix Biltmore Hotel in Phoenix awards wooden "WOW tokens" that are about the size of a half-dollar. Supervisors award tokens to employees who go the extra mile for guests or are "caught" doing a work task in a safe manner. Employees may redeem tokens for prizes starting at 20 tokens for movie passes for two, including soft drinks and popcorn. Other gift items include tickets for IMAX® Theatre, tote bags, company-identified merchandise such as a windbreaker for 100 tokens, and dinner for two at the Omaha Steak House for 150 tokens. One of the most popular token-rewards is a day off with pay for 200 tokens. The grand prize, a weekend for two at one of their resort hotels, takes 500 tokens and about one year to achieve for a hardworking, conscientious employee.

71. Reward new employees who stick with you for a specified period of time (six months or more) with a pair of Nike® shoes. This idea is particularly popular with teens and young adults in the hospitality industry where turnover is traditionally high.

72. Reward employees with an extra day of vacation.

73. Provide money for on-the-spot financial rewards whereby an employee can honor a co-worker for doing something that deserves special recognition.

74. If you believe your employees "work hard" so they can "play hard," why not offer an extra week of paid vacation immediately?

75. Award points throughout the year to employees for attendance and individual as well as team achievements. Employees can use the points to bid on gift items at an auction held at the end of the year.

76. Consider an R & R fund. When stockbrokers at Dean Witter Reynolds Inc. have a "bellringer" day, everyone wins. The successful brokers put $5 into the R & R fund with a maximum contribution of $25 in one month. Three or four times each year they use the money for social activities that include all employees.

77. Reward temporary employees with a framed certificate thanking them for their contributions to the company.

78. Transfer or purchase frequent flyer points for an employee's account.

79. During the holidays, reward employees with "Holly Money" that can be used to purchase company-identified merchandise or items in the company store, restaurant, or hotel.

80. If you supervise the finance department, hold an April 15th or end of the corporate fiscal year celebration as a reward for all their hard work.

81. Reward the employee with a personalized vehicle license plate.

82. Reward employees by inviting them to attend a national sales meeting or conference with their manager.

83. Give employees a day off with pay for their birthdays.

84. After a particularly hard shift (high volume, no breaks) reward your staff with a free meal.

85. Offer a variety of books from which an employee may select and keep a book as a reward.

86. If you own stocks and have an account with a brokerage firm, you can ask your broker to transfer one or more shares to an employee. It may not be a surprise because you will need the recipient's Social Security or taxpayer identification number, but it's a great reward idea.

87. Reward with software for an employee's home computer.

88. Pay for the initial membership fee and first month's membership dues to a local health club.

89. Keep top performers under constant review to be sure they're being rewarded and provided with plenty of training and development.

90. Promote from within whenever possible.

91. Offer the opportunity to job-share as a reward for good performance.

92. Arrange for an employee to spend a day with a sales representative. It's a great way to show appreciation as well as give the employee a chance to learn more about the business.

93. Allow a star salesperson the priviledge of not having to schedule any outside appointments for a day.

Chapter 3 - Camaraderie

Camaraderie in the workplace can be an important contributing factor to both productivity and low employee turnover. Employees that have the opportunity to get to know each other as individuals and to share food, laughter and ideas usually tend to perform better as a team. Developing camaraderie among employees, which includes managers, also contributes to a pleasant and productive atmosphere in the office. Even though some events may cut into the employees' "work time," the "dollar" cost to the company is generally small compared to the benefits.

1. Provide the food for "make your own" ice cream or yogurt sundaes.

2. Provide the food for "build your own sandwich" day.

3. Have the managers wash the employees' cars.

4. Employees or teams of employees design crossword puzzles using industry terminology. Hold a contest to determine winners of puzzle categories including most challenging, most typical of industry, most technical words used, most creative and funniest.

5. Eliminate problems with your software by holding a contest to eliminate defects. Have employees work together in teams. Award small prizes during the 6-week contest. Result: reduced backlog while building team spirit. (Cost-savings more than paid for this contest).

6. Start the day with a group sing-along.

7. Support employees in organizing an "Energizing Committee" to arrange for social events.

8. Designate a "VP of Fun" or "Minister of Happiness"—a position with responsibility for leading a committee that proposes social events, and is filled by employee vote.

9. Designate a wall where employees can exhibit their artwork or craft work for all to admire.

10. Send a team photograph with the words, "We proudly made this product," with every shipment the company makes.

11. Managers: Share your perks, such as tickets for ball games, fruit baskets and other gifts managers frequently receive, especially during the holidays. The people who work for you are often aware of such gifts even though you may not think so. Why not allow others to enjoy them too?

12. Establish a hotline so employees can share their hottest ideas. Record their messages so that everyone can access all the ideas at anytime.

13. Throw a mystery lunch party. Teams of employees have the fun of solving a mystery similar to that done in a mystery dinner theater.

14. Sponsor employees in foot races, walkathons, marathons or triathlons. Employees get a free T-shirt and the company helps build camaraderie.

15. Invite employees to submit their favorite recipes for inclusion in a company cookbook.

16. Set up a weaving loom that employees can collectively work on at their leisure to create a company wall hanging.

17. Hold a cookie exchange during the December holidays. Each employee who participates brings one dozen cookies to exchange. Everyone leaves with a variety of holiday treats.

18. Sponsor a flag football team. Provide logo T-shirts for each team member.

19. Hold monthly potluck theme lunches. Themes could be ethnic, country-western, Polynesian, low-fat, or "just salads."

20. Provide a meal prepared and served by the managers.

21. Have employees produce a video about their department.

22. Hold a hot soup slow-cooker party. Each employee who chooses to participate contributes one can or package of soup. All soups are mixed together for a wonderful potpourri of flavors. Serve with breads and beverages that may or may not be provided by the company.

23. Make a quotation book. When employees say something noteworthy, hear something they want to remember, or read an interesting quote, enter it into the book to share with all.

24. If you're redesigning the workspace, get employees involved in the actual design as well as selection of furniture, flooring covering, and wall color. Make the final result a team effort.

25. Have each department host an open house. All employees of the company are invited to attend. Serve coffee and cake or snacks and soft drinks to the guests.

26. A team collectively writes a poem about the work they're doing or on any subject related to who they are and what their roles are in the company.

27. "Secret Pal:" Each employee draws a name and that employee then becomes his or her secret pal for 3 months to 1 year. Pals surprise each other on birthdays, anniversaries with the company and for no reason at all throughout the year with a card or small gift. Hold a company function at the end of the year or sooner where secret pals reveal their identity to each other.

28. Provide space for employees to set up and grow herbs and spices year round.

29. Celebrate with a Founder's Day breakfast or lunch.

30. Provide space for a company band or chorus to practice.

31. Take employees to an indoor rock climbing facility. Take turns climbing the rock blindfolded while a partner calls out directions. It's fun and a great team building exercise.

32. Lend a bouquet of flowers: Bring a bouquet of flowers to work and give it to an employee with instructions to keep and enjoy it for 30 minutes (or one hour) then pass it on to another employee with the same instructions. You may wish to print instructions to go along with the bouquet.

33. Have employees wear their school or favorite team colors to work to kick-off the football season.

34. Hold a company-wide Olympic event. Employees compete in running, hurdles, cross-country, discus throw, etc.

35. The entire department takes a new employee to lunch on his or her first day at work just as is often done when someone leaves. What better way to help make the new employee feel welcome and give him or her a chance to get to know the rest of the team?

36. Employees nominate and vote for "supervisor of the year."

37. Is your team going to a meeting or holding a special event? Try this as a warm up. Select one individual to be the "clue master." Several days before the event is to take place, have each of the event participants send an e-mail to the "clue master" with a fact about themselves. This could be a past life event, a previous job, or an interesting hobby. Facts are compiled and associated with each participant by the "clue master." At the event, all participants receive at the same time a listing of all the facts. As participants mingle, they search to match facts with other individual participants. Participants should be cagey about giving up clues about their fact. At a prescribed time, the search stops. The person with the most correct answers wins the "Sherlock Holmes" prize, awarded by the "clue master."

38. Water Fights: At one volunteer fire department firefighters enjoy friendly competition in the form of water fights. Two teams of three people each aim fire hoses at a basketball located inside a fenced property. The first team to get the basketball past the other team's goal line wins. They also compete against other fire departments. The first place team wins $60.00.

Chapter 4 - Incentives for Growth

Sometimes employees need a little extra incentive to encourage them to grow. Employees who experience growth in their job or field of expertise become more valuable to the organization. They're usually happier as well. It's important for managers and business owners to encourage employees to reach their potential. There are numerous ways to offer incentives—many of them are quite simple but are often overlooked. Compensation isn't the only incentive. Employees want to feel they're part of the team and that the supervisor hears and considers their ideas and feelings. Encourage employees to grow and give them the opportunity to do so; both the employees and the company will benefit.

1. Invite employees to put their ideas about how to do things better into an "idea book."

2. Provide opportunities to taste the company's new products before they're introduced into the marketplace.

3. Surprise them with an upgrade in computer software.

4. Invite an employee to conduct a staff meeting in your absence.

5. Provide business cards for someone, such as a receptionist, who ordinarily wouldn't have them.

6. Schedule a brown bag "lunch and learn" workshop on personal development topics such as time management, diet and exercise, health, personal safety, or goal setting.

7. Include employees in a meeting they wouldn't ordinarily attend.

8. Provide employees with the opportunity to cross-train in another job in another department.

9. Help employees develop the skills needed to advance their careers.

10. Make it as hassle-free as possible to change jobs within the organization.

11. Support an in-house Toastmasters Club by providing meeting space and refreshments, and/or pay a portion of the annual dues for each employee that's a member.

12. Provide in-house instructors or pay tuition for employees to attend school to get their GEDs.

13. Offer "English as a second language" classes on company property before and/or after work.

14. Support a writers club both for employees who aspire to write as well as published authors.

15. Create a lending library. Employees and the company donate books to the employee-run library.

16. Send a postcard to the employee when you're out of town on business. Example: "John—Thank you for your support. Does this picture look like a market opportunity? With your help, they'll all be our customers too."

17. Hold a family day when each employee may bring a child to work to see what his or her parent does for a living.

18. Establish a mentor program. Match an entry-level manager with a higher level professional. All mentors must be volunteers because someone who is "required" to participate is usually not effective.

19. Re-deploy employees from downsized departments to expanding areas of the company rather than terminate their employment.

20. After 60 days of employment, top performers earn the use of a house charge account for business expenses.

21. Invite employees to participate in a new-hire orientation by explaining what goes on in their department.

22. Invite employees to participate in a company-paid, off-site seminar.

23. Teach employees how to juggle balls. Once they master juggling they can become instructors. Juggling is a great metaphor for mastering a variety of tasks.

24. Sponsor a "walk a mile in my shoes" day. Employees in various departments within the company get to experience firsthand what day-to-day activities keep their co-workers challenged. The goal is to increase respect among employees while promoting company awareness.

25. Provide a suggestion box. Implement the most valuable suggestions. Be sure to let your employees know you consider all of their ideas.

26. Have each team give themselves a name and create and display a coat of arms that represents every member of the team.

27. Plan a "First Day of Spring" party. Spring hails the beginning of a new season of growth.

28. Hold an office clean-up day. Everyone is dedicated to cleaning up their workspace as well as the common area. Celebrate afterwards with a luncheon for all.

29. If your company is listed on the stock exchange, hold "stock watch" meetings. It's a great motivator when employees gather to discuss how the stock is doing, especially if the company is doing well. Even if it isn't, it's a time to get together and discuss what the company/department is doing to reach its goals.

30. Offer flexible work hours during the summer.

31. Offer telecommuting. However, it needs a formal, written policy and support from upper management to make the difference between a commitment to working out the kinks or a transfer back to the office.

32. Invite a competent employee to write a set of instructions or a standard operating procedure.

33. Invite employees to participate in a company focus group regarding new products or a subject of concern or interest to everyone.

34. Have a "wish list" whereby employees can fill out what they want their next week's work schedule to look like. Supervisors try to honor requests as much as possible. This is especially useful in the hospitality industry.

35. Invite employees to have lunch with the president in the cafeteria or break room and ask any questions they want to ask. To eliminate fear or awkwardness, the questions go into a box and are drawn out and answered one by one until time is up.

36. Encourage arriving on time to staff meetings by asking the latest arrival to provide snacks for the next meeting. If everyone is on time, the manager or next most senior-ranking person buys for the next meeting.

37. Stretch assignments for high-potential employees. People who feel challenged are more likely to stay with you and grow with the company.

38. Offer career and expectation planning sessions. Even if your organization doesn't offer a formal program of this type, don't let it stop you from talking to your employees about their future plans.

39. Humanize the workplace by hiring people-oriented leaders. People who care about other people are the most likely to be successful in managing the work of others.

40. Delegate whenever possible. If you're not comfortable with delegating, make an effort to learn how. It's another way of letting your employees know that you trust them, as well as getting the work done.

41. Be sensitive to family issues. Show flexibility when an employee needs time off to attend a child's school or sporting event. Make concessions as needed for people without children, too. You'll find this idea to be an incentive for growth and long-term employment.

42. Offer continuous training and development opportunities. Don't be like the manager who said he didn't want his people trained because he lost them to his competition. Ignorance is a high price to pay. Encourage your employees to grow by offering on-going learning opportunities.

43. Set a good example. You can expect no more from those who work for you than you are willing to give yourself.

44. Provide a broad experience base of rotational assignments. Most people like variety. Give employees a chance to find out what it's like to work on different assignments in different parts of the organization.

45. Learn to give feedback without causing defensiveness. Everyone benefits when feedback is given in the helping spirit. Learn how to do this and your employees will have reason to grow with the company because they know you have their best interests in mind when offering criticism.

46. Focus on the results, not the rules. Don't punish employees by constantly reminding them about the rules and regulations. The results of their efforts are usually more important than how they reached their goals.

47. Promote new responsibilities, not promotions. There are times when there is no place to be "promoted to" in an organization. That's the time to take this idea to heart and get creative.

48. Learn how to build fun into your organization. Everyone enjoys a good time once in awhile. Find ways to have fun while you work. (See Chapter 6 for specific ideas).

49. If you own a restaurant, once a month invite the employee and his or her family for dinner in appreciation for excellent work.

50. Celebrate success! Everyone wants to work for a winning company. Applaud the achievements of your employees. Don't dwell on what hasn't happened; you can't change the past. Learn from both your mistakes and your successes and move on.

Chapter 5 - Freebies

Freebies are things you do for your employees for no particular reason. In contrast to recognition, awards and rewards, these are benefits that employees receive just because they're your employees. You're saying that you value them as employees on a day-to-day basis. You're giving them something that, while it may not cost the company much, can mean a lot to those who work for you. One of the things employees often silently resent is the "perks" that managers and higher level personnel receive. Let everyone in the company have a chance to enjoy an occasional "perk."

1. Set the coffee and soft drink vending machines on "free vend" for breaks, lunch, or even the day.

2. For lower wage earners with dependents, check out the advanced feature of the earned income tax credit (EIC). It requires the employee to complete a W-5 form annually. The benefit is an increase in pay without any net cost to the employee. (The extra pay is a Federal tax offset to the employer).

3. Lend money to employees through a formal, interest-free loan program.

4. Have a supply of postage stamps on your desk for the personal use of your employees.

5. Surprise employees with a continental breakfast.

6. Set up a complimentary gourmet coffee and tea station.

7. Keep the company refrigerator stocked with free soft drinks and juices.

8. Give employees discounts on merchandise the company sells.

9. Offer full or partial scholarships to employees' children.

10. Offer free haircuts.

11. Offer free manicures/pedicures.

12. Give the gift of personalized stationery or note cards.

13. Offer a free weekend or week in a company-owned timeshare.

14. In snow country, offer a ski-slope pass for a day.

15. In a printing firm: employees get anything they want printed for free as long as it's for personal use.

16. Offer 10-minute neck and shoulder massages on-site on company time. Have employees sign up in advance.

17. Provide free passes for public transportation.

18. Provide a reserved parking space at the airport "Park 'n Ride" so the employee always has a convenient place to park.

19. Implement "no-pay-day pay-days." On the week that employees don't receive a paycheck, hold drawings for small prizes.

20. Offer "VIC" days—a combination of vacation and sick days that employees may take with no questions asked.

21. Offer a coupon for a free lunch in the company cafeteria.

22. If you have college students working for you, pay to have a term paper typed for them.

23. Offer free flu shots.

24. Surprise your managers with a limousine to pick them up and take them to an off-site meeting.

25. Give gift certificates for food at Thanksgiving or Christmas rather than a turkey or ham. Employees may then purchase what they want, not what the company thinks they want.

26. Provide fresh fruit once a month for employees to enjoy at work.

27. Hold a "wellness day" and offer free blood pressure and cholesterol checks along with literature on health-related topics.

28. Give delivery drivers who use their own vehicles a free oil change or a free tank of gas.

29. Surprise employees with free drink tickets for airline flights.

30. Surprise employees with an airline ticket upgrade.

31. Provide a meal when employees volunteer to work overtime.

32. When employees are moved to a new area, i.e., department moves to a new floor/building, have balloon(s) tied to a bag of candy/cookies at each desk.

33. If your employees must pay for parking, give them an opportunity to earn free parking. It's a great way to give them a raise.

34. Provide free microwave popcorn and a microwave oven in which to pop it.

35. When the company upgrades its computer hardware and software, offer the old equipment and software to employees at nominal or no cost for home use.

36. Give your employees an attractive letter opener to help make opening mail more fun.

Chapter 6 - Fun Stuff

Let employees do something just for fun now and then. It can be a good way to help them feel their jobs are more than just a daily grind. Example: invite employees to wear "funky hats" to work one day; it can create a real "lift" in the work environment and doesn't cost anything dollar-wise. Employees spend a few minutes admiring each other's hats and have a good laugh or two to start the day.

Or you may decide to go a little further, such as renting a Kareoke® or video arcade machine. It's still worth the cost; employees who enjoy coming to work will likely be more productive than those who dread seeing their workplace each day. And a little laughter can go a long way in achieving that goal.

In addition, don't overlook the benefits of fun events that take place outside the workplace. Some of the following ideas may seem unusual, but they are being used or have been used in the past by at least one organization.

1. Hold a crazy shoelace or ugly tie day.

2. Hold a contest—guess the boss's weight in bagels.

3. Hold a blue jeans and T-shirt day.

4. Hire a graphologist to make a presentation on handwriting analysis. Give employees a chance to submit a sample of their handwriting to the instructor for feedback.

5. Sponsor a contest to design a computer-generated thank you card for customers/ clients.

6. Sponsor a paper airplane-flying contest.

7. Throw an "astronomy party" at an observatory. Invite employees and their family members to spend an afternoon or evening learning more about the universe.

8. Hold a "reverse" drawing. The last ticket called wins the grand prize; it doesn't have to be an expensive item.

9. Hold a Christmas tree ornament exchange.

10. Have an "Ugliest Christmas Tree Ornament" contest. Employees vote for the winning ornament. The winner gets a $10 gift certificate.

11. Turn the break room or cafeteria into a "cruise ship" with island decor, fruit punch, buffet lunch and the aroma of suntan oil.

12. Form a bingo club. Employees play bingo at lunch during the winter months. Award $5 bills to the winners.

13. Hold a "guess the lips contest" for Valentine's Day. All participants, both male and female, apply lipstick and press their lips to 3x5 cards. Cards are posted and everyone guesses which lips belong to whom.

14. Let employees bring a boom box to work and play music softly.

15. Have each department develop a theme game. Example: During Hospital Week, "guess how many syringes are in the jar" was a game one hospital department created to the delight of their co-workers.

16. Provide games (backgammon, chess, checkers, monopoly, and cribbage) in break rooms for employees to enjoy during their free time.

17. Hold an employee talent show. Sometimes they're more of a Gong Show, but they're fun.

18. Set up a swap-shop on a Saturday or a swap board at the office for employees to buy and sell sports equipment or other pre-owned items.

19. Designate a wall as "The Wall of the Absurd." Invite employees to post funny or absurd cartoons, quotes, actual memos, media articles, or jokes as long as they are not offensive in nature. You may want to have an employee committee approve postings on a weekly basis.

20. If your employees are especially creative, provide them with a floor cloth on which they can paint or draw during their breaks.

21. Set up a hobby room with basic equipment (workbenches, vices, and simple tools) and hold weekend classes taught by volunteer employee-instructors.

22. Throw a "toga party."

23. Planning an outside event in a park? Try Frisbee® golf. Set up a nine-hole course using large plastic laundry baskets that are numbered according to hole. Print up score cards with a layout of the course. Rules of golf apply. Any name brand Frisbee® is allowable. Set up teams and tournaments. Golf shoes are not required.

24. Invite employees to bring old ties and scarves to work and use them to make a wall hanging.

25. Hold a beer tasting party. Admission is a 6-pack of fine microbrewery beer per person or couple. The company provides the meeting place and the snacks. Feature a knowledgeable microbrewery brew master as a speaker.

26. Hold a wine tasting party. The company arranges for the tasting site and provides cheese and crackers. Admission is one bottle of fine wine per person or couple. Feature a knowledgeable vintner as a speaker.

27. Hold a contest to design a company bumper sticker. Leave the message to the imagination of your employees as long as it's not offensive.

28. Safety Bingo: Each employee has a bingo card. For each month that no one is injured on the job, draw three numbers. If there's an injury during the month, draw only one or two numbers. It takes several months, or more for someone to call "bingo" and win a small prize. This idea was shared by a manufacturing facility.

29. Sponsor a photo or art contest. All employees vote to determine winners in pre-determined categories.

30. Sponsor an ice skating party at an indoor rink for employees and their family members. This is especially fun in warm climates where people don't have much opportunity to ice skate.

31. Provide picnic tables for employees so they can eat outside in warm weather.

32. Hold a tailgate party in the company parking lot and invite employees and their families. Consider providing tours of the office or manufacturing facility for those who want to see where their spouse or parent works.

33. Provide a gumball machine with a supply of pennies or tokens so employees can help themselves any time.

34. Provide space for employees to plant and oversee gardens on company property. For example, one company in Atlanta provides space on the roof of their building.

35. Have casual days for one week if you're not already casual.

36. Hold a "theme day" where employees can wear costumes. Example: Clown Days, 50s or 60s Days, Hawaiian Days, Roaring Twenties Days, Western Days, Hobo Days, etc. Employees decorate, play music and have fun.

37. Hold a pumpkin-decorating contest—no carving, just drawing, dressing, etc. Or hold a carving contest if you prefer.

38. Hold a Halloween costume contest. Make it a theme party where everyone dresses like a storybook character or favorite celebrity.

39.　Employees dress in Halloween costumes and each department builds a haunted house. The children of employees are invited to trick-or-treat and visit the haunted houses from 5-7 p.m.

40.　Take a break from work and play childhood games like marbles, hopscotch, pick-up-sticks, jump rope, or jacks.

41.　Employees take turns starting a meeting with a joke, silly quote or funny story.

42.　Include "fun" in your company's core values that should already include respect, trust, excellence, balance, ethics, adaptability, empowerment, and risk taking.

43.　Set an aggressive time line for work so that there's scheduled time for officially sanctioned fun.

44.　Hold a hallway golf tournament in the office or plant. Let the employees build the course, but only with items that are already somewhere in the company. They may not bring anything from home.

45.　Hold a Harvest Ball in November and invite employees to come to work in old bridesmaid dresses and tuxedos.

46.　Organize an office pool for a sporting event, but no gambling. Winners get company-identified merchandise or other small gift items.

47.　Videotape employees at work and play, combine with music and run the finished tape on continuous play in the break room, cafeteria or other employee gathering place.

48.　Encourage employees to set up and care for tropical fish tanks they bring from home. It's a great way to provide a relaxing and fun environment for all.

49.　Sponsor an on-site dart ball contest.

50.　Hold an outrageous hairstyle or junky jewelry day.

51.　If you hear someone yell "bingo" while you're placing an order, it's not because of the total you just rang up. It's phone reps who answer the telephone playing "states bingo" while they punch in sales orders.

52.　Provide scented paper for lining office drawers.

53.　Price Waterhouse injects some light-hearted fun into their training course for entry-level consultants by including some elaborate role-playing. Instructors dress and act the parts of clients. Wearing funny hats and outlandish ties, the consultants create distinctive personalities, both agreeable and difficult.

54. Ask employees to come to a meeting with pictures and symbols and be prepared to describe the work they perform using these items.

55. Sponsor a clown clinic. Everyone has a chance to put on a clown face with special clown makeup. Encourage those who wish to wear a costume to do so.

56. Invite employees to share a hobby or special interest on a "show and tell" day.

57. Hold a mission statement signing party. Invite all employees to sign an enlarged version of the company mission statement. Then display it in the lobby or main entrance of the building.

58. Hold a "left foot day." Everyone wears the left shoe on the left foot and a mismatched shoe on the right foot.

59. Hold a pajama party where employees are invited to wear sleepwear to work.

60. Take employees on a nature walk. You may be surprised how much people know and are eager to share about their environment.

61. Set up table tennis or pool tables for employees to enjoy before and after work or during breaks.

62. Set up a trivia white- or blackboard where employees at their leisure can write trivia questions for others to answer as they walk by the board. It's fun and everyone has a chance to test his or her knowledge of trivia.

63. Hold a "bring your pet to work day."

64. Find out where your boss or the president shops and buy an exact same outfit. Wear it on the day after your boss does. This is especially effective if the boss is the opposite gender.

65. Manager does a "happy dance" dressed in an outrageous costume to celebrate a major achievement by the team.

66. Play laser tag off-and-on throughout the day.

67. Employees bring in their baby pictures to display. Everyone tries to guess who they are. The winner gets a baby bottle, pacifier or rattle.

68. Establish an "ugly tie rack." Place a sign on it that says: "Going to a job interview? Meeting with the boss? Borrow one of these if you need to."

69. Hold a picnic in the middle of winter in a snow-covered area. Play volleyball, grill burgers and toast marshmallows.

70. Throw a pizza-and-a-cartoon party. Employees can watch cartoons during lunch and enjoy pizza paid for by the company.

71. Hold a contest for employees' children. Invite them to write a story or draw a picture about their parents' jobs. Include the winners' art or essays in the company newsletter. Make a $100 donation to a charity selected by the winning child or children.

72. Hold a "snow day" in the middle of summer or in a warm climate where it never snows. A company in South Florida did. Requires acquiring snow or making your own.

73. Sponsor a flag football game in the snow.

74. Hold a "Who Can Dress in the Most Colors Day?"

75. Employees sponsor a children's carnival. Employees create all the events and supervise the activities that include face painting, carnival games with small prizes, clowns, jugglers, popcorn, and cotton candy.

76. Invite employees to bring to work and care for bird feeders and birdhouses. The company may wish to provide the bird food.

77. Hire an artist for a day or a long group-lunch to draw caricatures of your employees.

78. Make a ritual of photographing your team of employees once a year.

79. Hold a day of "Nerf Gun Warfare" (using Nerf® darts or torpedoes).

80. "Bonkers Day:" This is limited only by the creativity and imagination of your employees to decide what this day will be. Ideas are subject to final approval by management.

81. Throw a bowling party and invite employees and their families to bowl or simply relax and watch.

82. Provide art and craft supplies, (paints, chalk, pencils, paper, etc.), so that employees who choose to get creative during breaks, lunch, and before and after work can do so.

83. Take a bicycle horn into meetings. When discussion starts getting too somber, any team member can squeeze it and that signals it's time for everyone to get up and do jumping jacks.

84. Hold a tobogganing party. The company provides transportation by bus for the employees, or employees and their families to a local toboggan slope where hot chocolate and snacks are served throughout the afternoon or evening.

85. Hold an in-line skating clinic.

86. Manager wears a baseball uniform and cap and passes out popcorn at a staff meeting.

87. Take your employees to a virtual reality club for an afternoon or evening of fun.

88. Sponsor bowling, golf, softball, tag football and other team or league events.

89. Sponsor a forklift rodeo. If you have forklift drivers and haven't tried this safety awareness exercise, contact your truck supplier for information on how to get started.

90. Host a "gag day" once or twice a year. One or two people have the opportunity to buy a gag gift for each team member. It's done for fun, never to embarrass anyone. Gifts can range from a key chain for someone who always loses his keys to a gigantic pencil for the person who takes the most notes in a meeting. Other gag gifts might include an "I love to shop" T-shirt or a book on time management. Eventually everyone has a chance to select the gag gifts.

91. Hold a kite-flying contest with categories such as the highest flying, most colorful, most unusual, longest in the air, and first to crash.

92. Hold a bake-off with specific categories such as brownies, breads, cakes, pies, and cookies.

93. Send employees on a scavenger hunt on company property or to an off-site location. Provide each team with a disposable camera to photograph the items they find that are on the list. Have the film developed within one hour while employees share tales of the fun of the adventure.

94. Encourage employees to stand on their desks when they need a break.

95. Hold a "Muffin Friday" every month. Employees sign up for a Friday when they will provide the muffins, sweet rolls and/or bagels for everyone. Employees arrive at work 15 minutes early to enjoy the goodies.

96. Provide meeting space for an investment or book club.

97. Get to work before your employees arrive and leave small surprises such as a candy bar, key chain, company identified merchandise in the form of caps or T-shirts in each employee's work area.

98. Provide a "dunking booth" at the company picnic. Managers and supervisors take turns sitting in the booth, much to the delight of their employees who try their best to "sink" their bosses.

99. For $39.95, Personal Passions (a publishing company) will personalize a romance novel about one of your employees. Although the novel itself is pre-written, the publisher customizes each book by inserting things like their name, hair color and even favorite drink into the text. Find Personal Passions' web site at http://www.emerald-seduction.com/.

100. Hold a "catch and release" fishing contest with prizes given for the person that catches the largest fish, smallest fish, most colorful and most unusual fish.

101. Take employees on a go-cart outing.

102. Hold a pet photo contest. Judge photos in different categories such as most unusual pet, largest and smallest pets, most animated face, or even the pet that looks most like its owner.

103. Provide an assortment of picture puzzles in the employee breakroom.

104. Provide plastic spoons dipped in chocolate and hardened to use with coffee. Chocolate sticks for stirring coffee (raspberry is especially tasty) are also a nice treat.

105. Surprise employees with a bottle of bubbles for blowing. Enjoy the day blowing bubbles with your employees or consider a bubble-blowing contest.

106. Arrange for a surprise picnic in the company parking lot.

107. Provide space for a company-sponsored rummage sale on a Saturday. Open to the public, the event gives employees a chance to sell unwanted items as well as shop the bargains offered by their co-workers.

108. Take your employees bowling for Thanksgiving using frozen 10 to 20 pound turkeys as bowling balls. The winners get the turkeys to take home.

109. Throw an "Elvis Sighting" party. Employees dress like Elvis and prizes are awarded for the best look-alike. Decorate, play Elvis music and encourage employees to bring Elvis memorabilia to display.

110. Set up a lending library of audio and videotapes.

111. Remember hula-hoops? Why not hold a contest to see who can "hoop it up" the longest?

112. Hold a contest to guess the date of the first snowfall or first day when the temperature reaches 100 degrees.

113. Big Foot: Everyone traces their foot on a piece of paper. Post them and everyone guesses which foot belongs to whom. Gag gifts may also be awarded for the longest foot, shortest foot, widest foot, narrowest foot and funniest-looking foot.

114. Let employees paint and decorate the restroom(s). One business owner was surprised (shocked) to find the restroom in his retail store painted lime green.

115. Hold a bicycle limbo contest. This idea came from a bicycle shop owner whose employees enjoy riding bicycles under limbo poles. He said it's amazing to watch.

116. Give all employees a yo-yo when the company stock recovers from a major loss.

117. Surprise your employees with a pancake breakfast.

118. Have all employees exchange jobs with each other for a day.

119. Throw a company party. However, everyone comes dressed for the prom.

120. Take your employees to a paintball parlor.

121. Take your employees on a tubing trip on a hot summer day.

122. Declare a "Fun Day" and plan special fun events throughout the day.

123. Everyone draws the name of a co-worker that they keep secret. However, they must act like that person for the rest of the day.

124. Take a break and everyone plays shuffleboard.

125. Hold a "polka dot" day. Everyone dresses in polka dots. A prize is given for the person wearing the most dots.

126. Develop a "fun calendar." Schedule fun events on a regular basis and get your employees involved in carrying them out.

127. Sponsor a basketball game—employees versus their supervisors. Everyone dresses in wild and wacky clothing. The game is held in a company, community or high school gymnasium after work. Employees' families are invited to attend along with co-workers.

128. For the employee who puts out the most "fires" during the month, give him or her a miniature fireman's hat or toy fire truck.

129. Hire magicians to wander throughout the building during employee breaks and lunch. It's spontaneous and fun. It also gives you a chance to preview magicians for use at a company function later in the year.

130. Hold a progressive lunch. Food is provided by employees. Start at one department with hors d'oeuvres, progress to the next department for soup or salad, the next department for the main course and the last department for dessert.

Chapter 7 - Community Spirit

Most companies recognize the importance of participation in charitable and community events. They often make donations of money, products or services to support such activities. The most valuable contribution of all, however, is your employees' individual efforts. Encourage employees to join in or contribute to these endeavors. Most people like to help others. Arrange for your employees to get directly involved with the people they're helping. For example: "Adopt" a family for the holidays and provide them with food and gifts they might not otherwise be able to afford.

Support employee participation in community events by letting them have time at the office to organize and sponsor such things as the "Angel Tree" mentioned in this chapter. Also, acknowledge their efforts on behalf of others. Many organizations publicize volunteers' work or present plaques or certificates to volunteers. Consider a simple write-up in the company newsletter about the employee's work on behalf of a non-profit organization. Or you may choose to encourage volunteer work by offering an incentive, such as an extra day of vacation.

Although the holiday season is a time when many people think about charity, don't forget about the rest of the year. Schedules aren't as hectic and many charities are begging for support. The community, company and employees win when employees work together to help others.

1. Hold a white elephant gift exchange in lieu of a holiday gift exchange. Money that would have been spent on purchased gifts goes to charity.

2. Match your employee's monetary donation to a charitable organization and get a tax write-off as well. For example, a fisherman got the company he worked for to match his contribution to a "Fishing Has No Boundaries" program in his community.

3. Donate money to public television in the name of your employees.

4. Consider paid time-off for employees who work as telephone volunteers for fundraisers such as charity telethons, or public television or radio events.

5. Arrange for employees to appear on a local telethon to present a monetary gift on behalf of the company and its employees to a charity such as one that conducts medical research on muscular dystrophy, cerebral palsy, multiple sclerosis, heart disease or cancer.

6. Help stock your community food pantry with food items or cash donations.

7. Sponsor employees in a walk or run for charity.

8. Hold a silent auction for charity. Donated items may be new or used.

10. Encourage your team of employees to become "bell ringers" for the Salavation Army during the Christmas holidays to raise money for the needy.

11. Collect used books and magazines for distribution to nursing homes and hospital waiting rooms.

12. Encourage your employees to practice "reach-out rituals" by keeping in touch with the elderly, or maybe volunteering for Meals on Wheels once a quarter.

13. Allow employees to repair computers on company time, up to a certain limit. Donate computers to local schools.

14. Sponsor a food/clothing drive for the homeless.

15. Support employees that volunteer to prepare and serve meals in a homeless shelter.

16. Have employees decorate a Christmas tree to donate to a hospital for their lobby.

17. Make tabletop holiday decorations for nursing home residents.

18. To encourage employees to pursue charitable endeavors, give employees a certain number of paid leave hours every year to do volunteer work in the community.

19. Provide a Christmas tree to be called the "Angel Tree." Ask employees to donate specific items such as a gift box containing one hair shampoo, one hair conditioner, one toothpaste, one toothbrush and one hand lotion. For each package of items or gifts donated, employee receives a paper angel. Most employees tend to proudly display the angels in their work area, showing that they were a contributor.

20. Have employees build a "wishing well" with all the money collected donated to charity.

21. Offer "casual days for charity." Employees pay to wear blue jeans to work for a specific period of time and the money goes to charity.

22. Hold a bake sale or other fundraiser for an employee or an employee's family member that has extraordinary medical or living expenses because of illness.

23. "Lend" an employee to the United Way for the period of their fundraising campaign in your community.

24. Have an on-site blood drive. Coordinate this with your community blood bank. Consider giving employees who donate blood one-half day off with pay.

25. Adopt a highway. Take your team on a Saturday to clean up a stretch of highway near the work site or any place in the community that needs help. Provide soft drinks and snacks or sandwiches.

26. Some progressive nursing homes allow visiting pets as a way to boost life interest among residents. Sponsor a "take your pet to visit senior citizens" day. This could be a regular, on-going program throughout the year or a one-time event.

27. Be a corporate sponsor of a foreign exchange student.

28. At the end of the year hold an auction for items that were made in the company hobby shop. All money goes to charity.

29. Promote a drive to collect used eyeglasses. Donate them to the local Lions Club for recycling.

30. The U.S. Marine Corps Reserve Toys for Tots Program is directed by the Commander, Marine Forces Reserve and his staff from the Marine Forces Reserve Headquarters in New Orleans, Louisiana. The Commander, Marine Forces Reserve has, under his command, 187 Marine Corps Reserve Units located in 46 states, the District of Columbia, and Puerto Rico. Each Reserve Unit and approved MCL Detachment conduct toy collection and distribution campaigns in the communities surrounding their Reserve Center or Detachment headquarters each year. Campaigns begin in October and last until December 22. Local business leaders play a key role by allowing Marines to locate collection receptacles in their stores. Businesses provide free warehouse space during October, November and December for storing and sorting toys. They also provide vehicles in which to collect toys from collection sites, sponsor toy and fund raising events and help Marines receive maximum media exposure for Toys for Tots. For more information on how you can help call 703-640-9433.

31. Sponsor a foster child in a third world country and challenge the other departments in the company to do the same.

32. Arrange for a company representative to participate in a high school career fair or to speak in a classroom of an employee's child.

33. Donate 2-5% of your profits to non-profit organizations in your community. If you're a retailer, place a sticker on selected merchandise that will support a given charity.

34. Hold a drive to collect used bicycles for needy kids at Christmas. Bikes are repaired and/or cleaned by employees before distribution to charities.

35. Collect used greeting cards for St. Jude's Born Again Recycling Program. St. Jude's Ranch for Children is a Nevada community focusing on the needs of abused, abandoned and neglected children of all races and faiths. Children take the front of greeting cards of all occasions (not limited to Christmas), glue them to preprinted card backs, and sell the "new" cards to the public. Donors should send card fronts only, with no writing on the reverse and that can be trimmed to fit 5-by-7-inch card backs. Send to: St. Jude's Ranch for Children, 100 St. Jude's St., Boulder City, NV 89005-1618. Those wishing to buy Born Again Cards can send $6.50 for a package of 10 to the ranch at P.O. Box 60100, Boulder City, NV 89006-0100. Use the same address for any other correspondence. For credit card purchases, call 1-(800) 492-3562. For other information call 702-294-7124.

36. Los Medicos Voladores (LMV), also known as the "Flying Doctors," was founded in 1974 to provide health services and education to the people of northern Mexico. LMV's primary purpose is to send medical teams on 4-day trips to Mexico each month. Teams include a pilot, translator, medical professional (usually MD, dentist, optometrist or chiropractor) and possibly a co-pilot or general volunteer. Donations from individuals, companies and service organizations help members purchase medical, dental, and health care supplies, clinic and communications equipment. For more information about volunteering or where to donate equipment, supplies or money, call Los Medicos Voladores at (800) 585-4LMV.

37. Operation Smile is the not-for-profit, volunteer medical service organization that provides re-constructive facial surgery to indigent children and young adults in 16 developing countries and in the United States. Based in Norfolk, Va., Operation Smile provides education and training to physicians and other health care professionals. Since 1982, Operation Smile has treated 45,000 children here and abroad, with one cleft lip surgery costing approximately $750. For information on how your organization can help call 1-888-op-smile.

38. On Feb. 2, 1999, half a million students across America were paired with workplace mentors as part of a nationwide initiative called Groundhog Job Shadow Day. The idea is for students to spend a half a day in a mentored work site shadowing an employee as he or she goes through a normal day on the job. In 1998 on Groundhog Job Shadow Day, close to 400 students in three states shadowed employees in restaurants and hotels. In 1999, the National Restaurant Association joined forces with the American Hotel & Motel Association and the Hospitality Business Alliance to get students involved in shadowing employees in restaurants and hotels in all 50 states. Call them at (800) 424-5156, ext. 3679, or leave a message. Groundhog Job Shadow Day is a joint effort of America's Promise (headed by General Colin Powell), the American Society of Association Executives, Junior Achievement, and the National School-to-Work Office.

39. Volunteers are needed at Ronald McDonald Houses to answer phones, talk with parents, work on projects with staff members, or comfort a child. They also need people to help produce the major house events like golf and tennis tournaments or

help wrap gifts for donations during the holidays. Supper volunteers provide and coordinate a meal. Garden volunteers maintain the grounds at the Ronald McDonald House. Other volunteers provide such services as leading art projects, presenting plays for children, or helping with sing-alongs.

Chapter 8 - Outrageous!

I've intentionally left this chapter for last. After reviewing all of the ideas for recognizing, rewarding and retaining good people, there were four ideas that seemed to have no place. Because they were so outrageous, I decided to create a chapter just for them.

I was speaking at a conference in February 1998 when I asked this question of the audience: "What do you do to keep good people in your business motivated to work for you?" A man in the back of the room waved his hand. I hurried to him with a microphone and repeated the question. He responded with the first entry for this chapter. Later, a second idea came up when a man in one of my audiences in Orlando volunteered his idea. A third and fourth entry followed.

I invite anyone with outrageous ideas to submit them so that Chapter 8 can be completed.

1. Streak! Take off all of your clothing and run around the building. The man from South Africa who does this says his employees love it! He streaks every time his employees meet their goals for the month.

2. All the men in a retail store changed clothes, dressed up in drag, and partied at a local bar after work.

3. A startup company held a "Romp in the Nude in the Snow Day." Employees enjoyed getting wild and crazy for a brief time on a Saturday. Pizza and beer was served after the follies.

4. Hire a tattoo artist to create tattoos on the bodies of gutsy employees.

Do you have an idea you would like to share with others? This book will be updated with each printing. If we use your idea in a new edition, you will receive a complimentary copy of that edition.

Send ideas to:

Carol A. Hacker & Associates
209 Cutty Sark Way
Alpharetta, GA 30005
Phone - 770-410-0517
Fax - 770-667-9801
CarolAHacker@hotmail.com

Be sure to include your name, address and telephone number (daytime and/or evening number). Also, we need to know whether your idea has actually been used or is an idea you think would work but hasn't been tried before.

Other Books by Carol

Job Hunting in the 21st Century—Exploding the Myths, Exploring the Realities, St. Lucie Press, 1999.

Misconceptions about the job-hunting process have sabotaged the attempts of many job seekers. This book is about how to maintain the competitive edge in a business climate where the jobless rate has slipped to a 28 year low. It brings the reader up to date on the realities of understanding and mastering the job search process. It provides concepts that are easy to apply and presents the most current information on how to find a job in today's job market. It examines the most common job hunting myths and offers solutions for avoiding the pitfalls associated with each.

The Costs of Bad Hiring Decisions & How to Avoid Them 2nd Edition, St. Lucie Press, 1998.

This book is loaded with practical, easy-to-read, and understand tips for making sound and defensible hiring decisions. Learn how to keep your employment decisions healthy and profitable. From deciding what you're looking for in a candidate, to extending a job offer, this book will prove to be your on-the-shelf consultant.

Hiring Top Performers—350 Great Interview Questions For People Who Need People, 1998 revised. BEST SELLER!

Ideal for businesses of all sizes, in all industries, this book offers 350 sample interview questions to help you get the information needed to make good hiring decisions. It's written in clear language and offers practical guidance to hiring managers at all levels.

The High Cost of Low Morale ...and what to do about it, St. Lucie Press, 1996.

Morale is an elusive quality. It's a feeling that's created within every employee. When morale is high, it's worth its weight in gold. When morale is low, the cost is tremendous. Dozens of interviews with top business leaders reveal inside tips for keeping good employees motivated to do their best. Time-tested advice for leaders will help keep your team energized and on track.

Two of Carol's Most Popular Workshops

How to Compete in the "War for Talent"

Tired of fighting for good people? Is your team's performance a casualty of high turnover? Learn how to eliminate hiring decisions that are costing your business thousands! The average price of a regrettable choice can easily be one-third or more of the annual salary. If you're sick of employees who shine in the interview but tarnish quickly once employed, this workshop is for you. Never again transfer, promote or hire without being sure you're making the right decision the first time. Your attendance at this workshop will allow you to learn first-hand how to:

- Develop a broad-based sourcing strategy that balances the time it takes to hire with cost-per-hire.
- Insure a quality pool of top-notch candidates from which to choose.
- Recruit the right people, with the right skills, for the right jobs.
- Determine if candidates can do what they claim they can do.
- Decide what to ask and not ask to stay out of legal hot water.
- Get references to speak candidly, even in a litigation-happy society.

21st Century Strategies for Gaining Employee Loyalty and Reducing Turnover

This workshop offers state-of-the-art strategies for keeping your talent base, even in a tight job market. Low unemployment combined with increasingly aggressive recruiting has made retaining good people more and more difficult. Successful businesses have a strategic competitive advantage when reducing turnover; it's the key to satisfied and loyal customers. If you're looking for innovative, straightforward methodologies for retaining top talent, this workshop is a must-attend! Part of what you will learn is how to:

- Analyze the marketplace to find out why you're losing good people to the competition.
- Use new-hire orientation to reinforce your business as the employer of choice.
- Align and develop the next generation of leaders with the company's strategic plan and objectives.
- Give critical feedback and still build employee loyalty, increase productivity and boost profits.
- Use exit interview data to help identify major contributing factors to turnover.

48

NOTES

NOTES

NOTES